Kenneth Fuchs

Falling Canons

for Piano

ISBN 978-1-4803-6731-9

Exclusively Distributed By

7777 W. Bluemound Rd. P.O. Box 13819 Milwaukee, WI 53213

www.ebmarks.com
www.halleonard.com

Piano

for Christopher O'Riley

Falling Canon No. 1
(Canon at the Unison)

KENNETH FUCHS

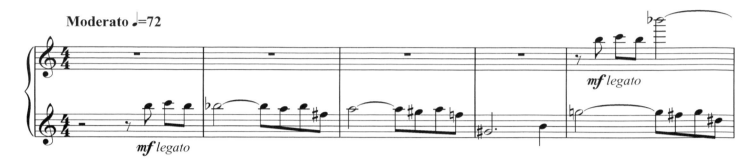

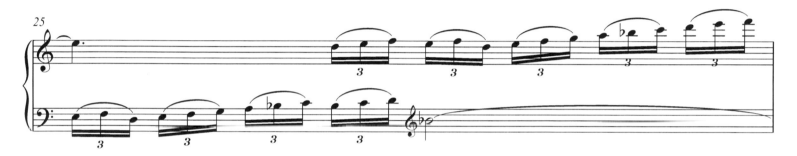

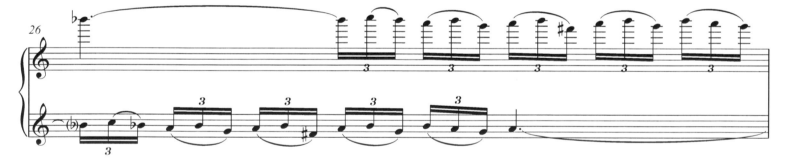

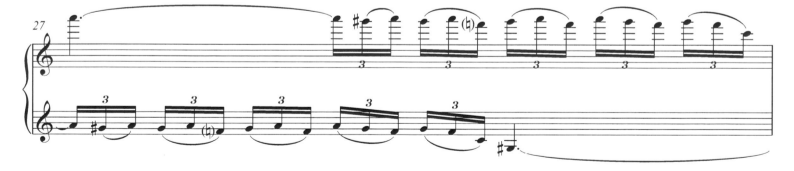

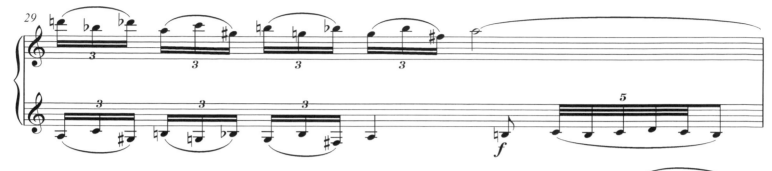

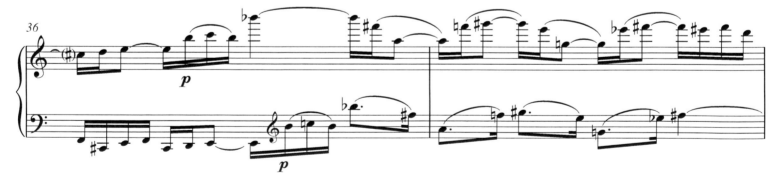

Falling Canon No. 2
(Canon at the Second)

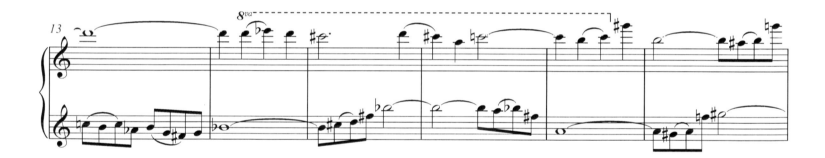

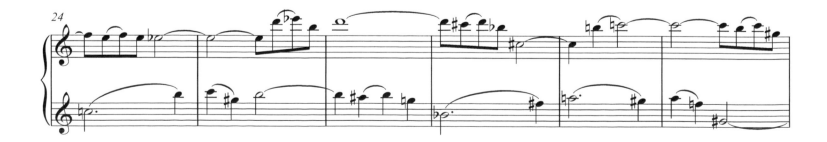

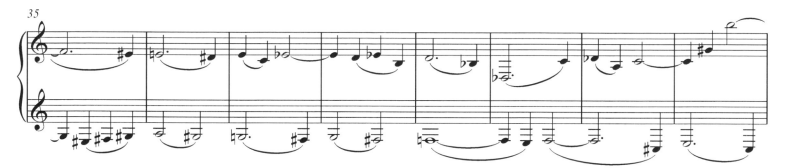

[1'39"]

Falling Canon No. 3

(Canon at the Third)

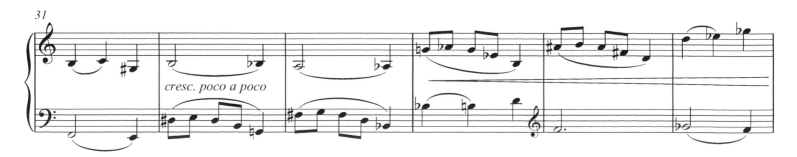

73

79

85

91

97

104
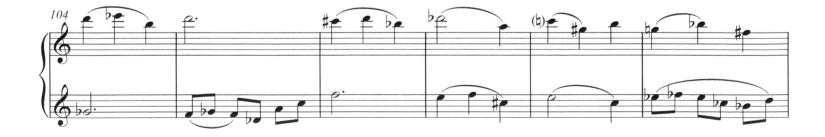

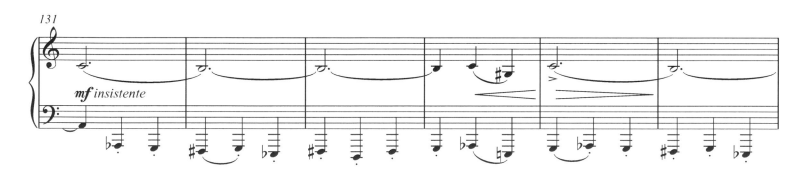

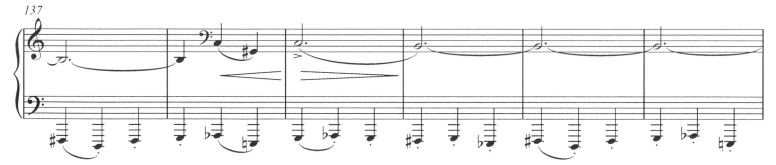

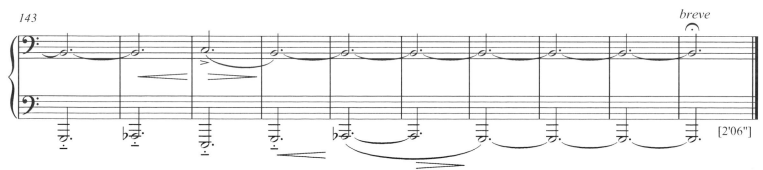

[2'06"]

Falling Canon No. 4

(Canon at the Fourth)

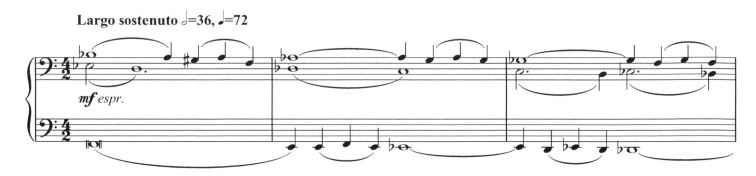

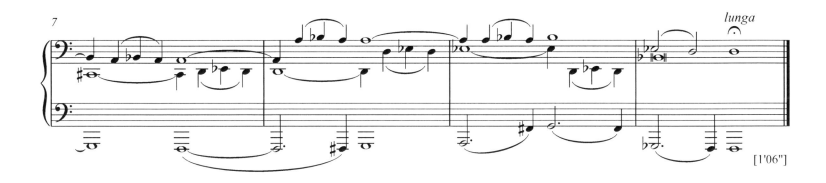

[1'06"]

Falling Canon No. 5
(Canon at the Fifth)

Veloce e ritmico ♩=144

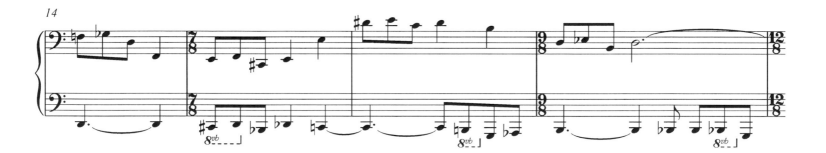

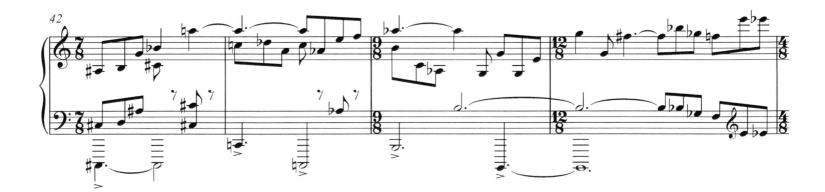

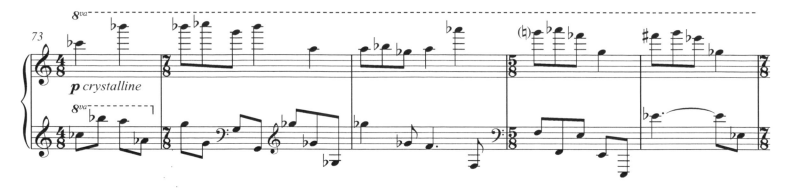

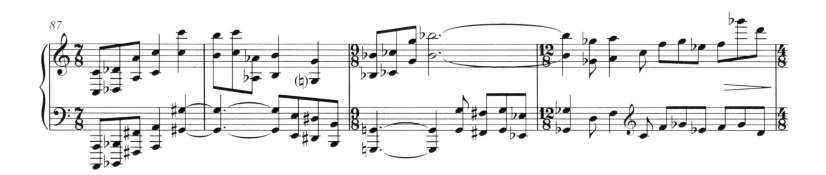

[2'44"]

Falling Canon No. 6

(Canon at the Sixth)

Largo misterioso ♩=72

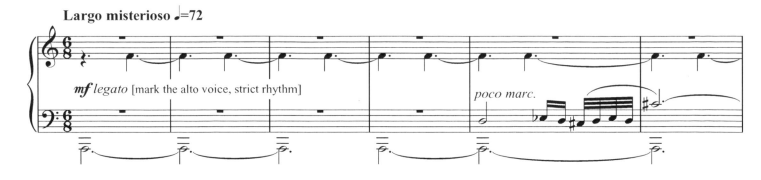

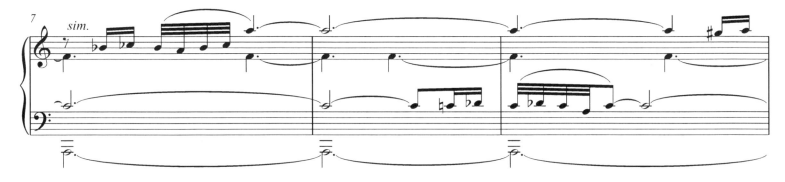

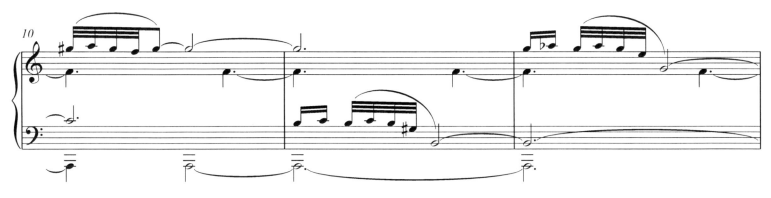

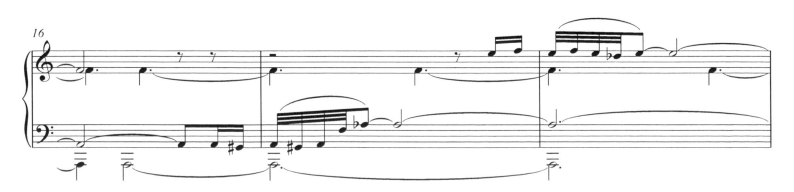

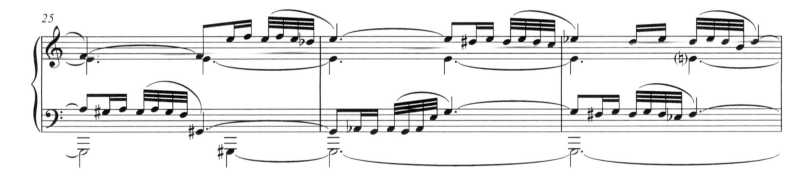

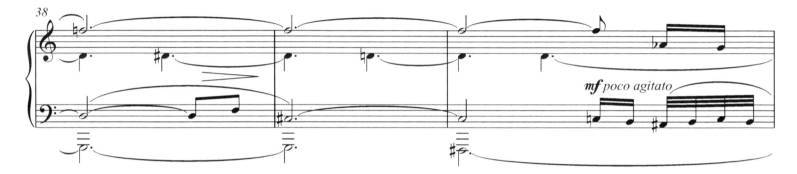

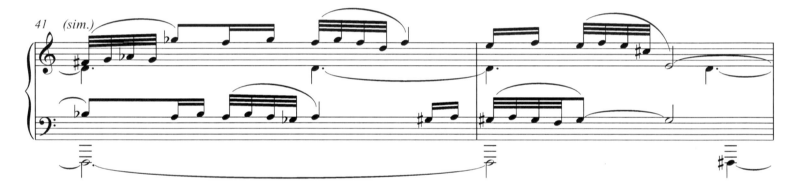

[2'47"]

Falling Canon No. 7
(Canon at the Seventh)

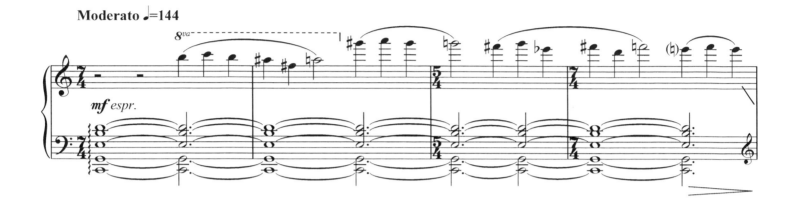

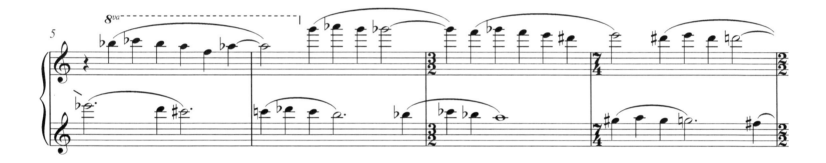

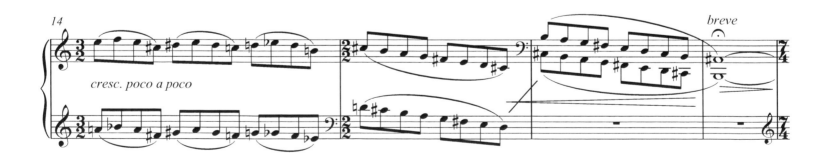

18 **L'istesso tempo**

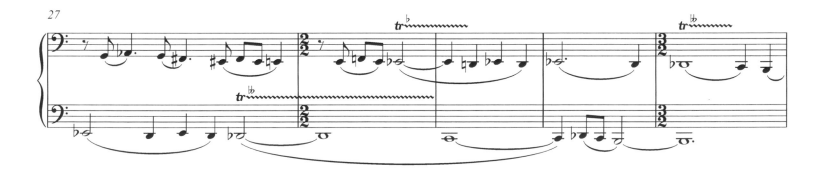

Misurato, l'istesso tempo

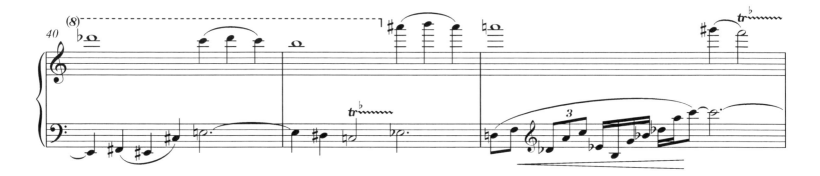

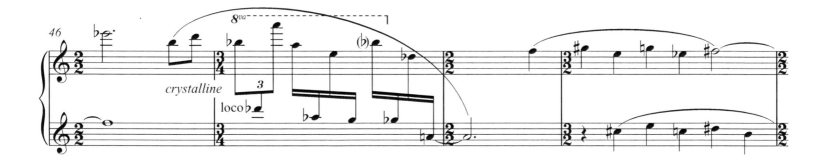

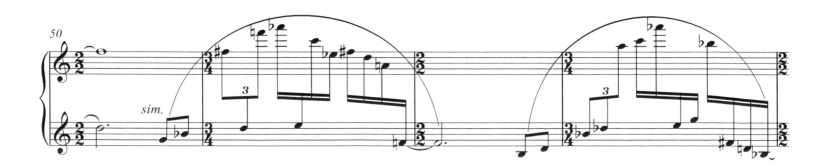

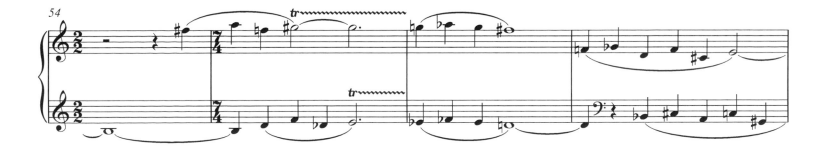

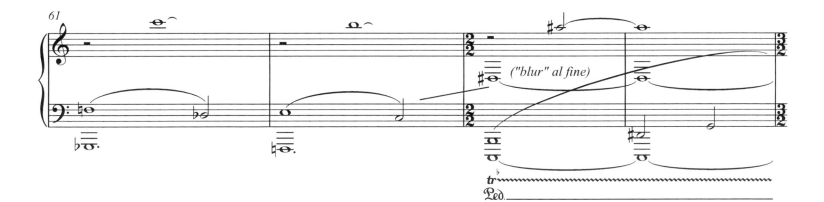

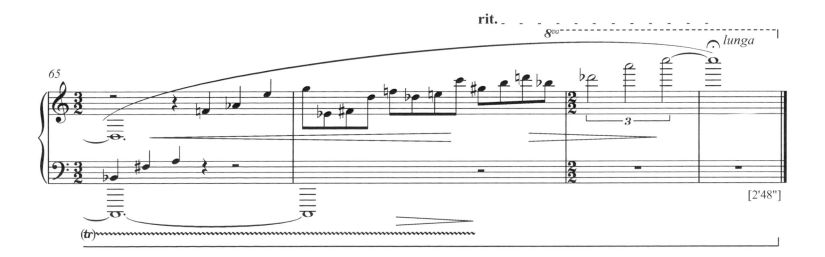

[2'48"]

for Christopher O'Riley

*F*alling Canons grew out of compositional elements from *Falling Man*, an extended scena for baritone voice and orchestra that I composed between 2008 and 2010. The original vocal text, adapted for setting by J. D. McClatchy, is based on a fragment from Don DeLillo's powerful post-9/11 novel *Falling Man*, published in 2007.

During the composition of *Falling Man*, I found that there were contrapuntal elements in the music that I could explore further and distill in the pure medium of solo piano. The original *Falling Man* theme is organized around a sequence of 12 different descending pitches. The compositional manipulation of the theme's 12 pitches in the vocal-orchestral work does not strictly adhere to classic dodecaphonic procedures — the pitches and their permutations are taken up in various melodic and harmonic combinations and provide the basis for musical development and transformation over the course of a through-composed vocal aria interspersed with vocal recitatives and orchestral interludes.

The development of the compositional material in *Falling Canons* is much more rigorous, the goal being to explore the essence of the *Falling Man* theme on the keyboard within limited musical parameters.

The interval of canonic imitation, temporal relationships, and the time signature of each canon are related to the sequential number of each piece. Each of the seven canons begins and ends on a unifying primary pitch. Each unifying pitch represents a degree of the C major scale. The first canon is pitched on B, the second canon is pitched on A, the third on G, and so forth until all seven pitches of the scale are represented in a descending fashion. The seventh and final canon is pitched on C.

Following is the compositional design of the set of seven canons:

Canon No. 1 (at the unison; pitched on B; 4/4)

Canon No. 2 (at the second; pitched on A; 2/2)

Canon No. 3 (at the third; pitched on G; 3/4)

Canon No. 4 (at the fourth; pitched on F; 4/2)

Canon No. 5 (at the fifth; pitched on E; 5/8)

Canon No. 6 (at the sixth; pitched on D; 6/8)

Canon No. 7 (at the seventh; pitched on C; 7/4)

Duration: approximately 15 minutes

— Kenneth Fuchs

World première: July 30, 2010
Christopher O'Riley, piano; Caramoor Center for Music and the Arts, Katonah, New York